Diary
of a Fool

JOHN P. DIMARZIO

ISBN 979-8-88644-852-8 (Paperback)
ISBN 979-8-88644-853-5 (Digital)

Covenant Books
11661 Hwy 707
Murrells Inlet, SC 29576
www.covenantbooks.com

Preface

When I first decided to write this book, I told my son, "I am going to write a book called *Diary of a Fool.*" He said jokingly, of course, "Is it an autobiography?" My first thought was, *You smart aleck.* Then I realized that this book is just that. It is an autobiography of who we can become. We will see what the fool does, how he thinks, and how he reacts. So be cautious. This may be your autobiography.

The purpose of this book is not just to see folly in others but to help us avoid the pitfalls of foolishness. It also reveals how not to live life in the foolish lane. Foolishness takes its toll in many ways. It subjects us to the scrutiny of others and can leave us morally and spiritually bankrupt. In the pages we will see attributes, actions, and intentions of the foolish one. There is a place for guest reflection post. Please reflect on the day and include in this post what you may be thinking, feeling, or desiring in your own life based on the day's reflection.

A special thank you to my daughter, Elizabeth VanNatta, who has been my go-to person.

Introduction

Hello! My name is Fool. I would like to invite you into my world. I will share with you a diary of my approach to life and daily activities. First, understand a fool is one who does foolish things. However, not everyone who does foolish things is necessarily a fool. As a fool, I am locked into a mindset beginning with my disbelief or lack of fear in God. Therefore, I function in that mode. This book does not define a fool. As a fool, I define myself by my actions through process and intentions or lack thereof. You will also see in me a fool that is one who tries to fool others but fools only himself. You will further note I am described by my concepts and attributes in the Scriptures. The purpose is to help you see, understand, and avoid me or being like me.

Caution

Do not fall into the trap of labeling others. That is God's call, not ours.

Day 1

THE FOOL IS ONLY ROWING WITH ONE OAR

The fear of the LORD is the beginning of knowledge,
but *fools* despise wisdom and instruction.

—Proverbs 1:7

Dear believing friends, *for your information,*

Today I will be very busy. I have my life figured out. To think I need the intervention of someone I cannot see is ridiculous. I can fend for myself. The only fear I have is the fear of your continual pestering me. I do not like people telling me what to do or what to believe. I will learn from my personal experiences. After all, I am wise, like, nothing bad has happened to me.

Dear fool,

You begin your day with no end in sight. Your life is an endless venture of wandering in the abyss of your mind. Today, you encountered knowledge. Knowledge tried to befriend you, but you would have none of that. Knowledge tried to give you direction, but you were too busy. You fear knowledge more than you fear the giver of knowledge. Today was a wash for you—no hits, no runs, and plenty of errors. Your hatred was displayed by your intolerance for anyone who knew where they were going and what they believe. Fool, understand we open the door of understanding when we listen to someone wiser and there is someone wiser than you.

Guest reflection post:

Day 2

THE FOOL DRIVES WITH THE BRAKES ON

The *fool* says in his heart, "There is no God." They are corrupt, their deeds are vile; there is no one who does good.

—Psalm 14:1

Hey, diary. This is my second day tolerating believers. They still haven't changed my mind.

Hey, world. I cannot hear, feel, touch, or see God. Why should I believe he exists? Those of you who do are not any better off. Your house is not any bigger, your cars any better. What advantage do you have? I question your veracity. You act like you are so sure of your belief and destiny. Big deal. Where was God when you were in the hospital or when your identity was stolen? I do not need to explain anything to you. I do what is best for me. If I need something, I take it. Not believing God exists removes all my moral inhibitions and limitations. I adjust my view as necessary. I avoid anyone or anything that challenges my disbelief. I am one free individual. I think. I have no concerns about the future. I live for today.

The above passage is also appropriate to understanding the fool's philosophy. Therefore, it is labeled "day two." Solomon leads the way by putting the fool in the headlights. Major concern—fools despise knowledge and instruction because it offends them. Fools are offended by that which is appreciated by others. Foolishness opens the door to mediocrity. Those who invest nothing can expect nothing. The fool rows with one ore.

Dear fool,

Please realize all knowledge has a source of origin. That source serves as a foundation of which we build our beliefs. From this source, principles evolve that confirm or contradict how we live. There are two primary sources of origin for knowledge—God or man. If we don't choose God's wisdom, we are left to man's speculation. To fear the Lord infers there is a respect due him because he is creator of the universe and the source of all knowledge. Those foolish enough to refuse God's wisdom do not want a discipline that makes them accountable. Want wisdom daily? Go back to the beginning—God.

Guest reflection post:

Day 3

THE FOOL IS A KNIFE LICKER

The lips of *fools* bring them strife, and their mouths
invite a beating. The mouths of *fools* are their undoing,
and their lips are a snare to their very lives.

—Proverbs 18:6

Diary, my memoirs and actions speak for themselves. I feel trapped. Stop picking on me.

Often, self-inflicted wounds are not realized until after they happen. One must ask the question, "Are your words life-threatening, and are you putting your existence in jeopardy with your mouth?" The fool does this on several fronts when he causes division, "strife," and when he separates people. Two people will put him on their hit list. Next, when he threatens others, he invites retaliation. Then when he uses his mouth to say more than necessary, he loses his creditability (i.e., his "undoing"). Finally, in his efforts to ensnare others, he traps himself. Take a lesson from the fool. Do not separate people, threaten them, multiply unnecessary words, or try to entrap others. Your lips, your mouth, and your tongue will be an avenue of blessing, not a source of a pummeling.

Guest reflection post:

Day 4

BARNEY FIFE TO THE RESCUE

A fool finds no pleasure in understanding but delights in airing his own opinions.

—Proverbs 18:2

Diary, it's day four. Time to snore. I am getting tired of trying to reason if they would just listen to me. They might learn something.

Our opinions may be intuitive to us, but that is just what they are—opinions. They should be aired with extreme caution and only when asked for. We align ourselves with the foolish when we find pleasure in hearing ourselves expound that which impresses only ourselves. Giving more credibility to our opinion than to honest evaluation of a matter is what Solomon is addressing. The pleasure derived from understanding is an ability to deal with the truth in a forthright way. Opinions are personal tools to advance our thinking process, not to replace truth or to be used for obnoxious ego trips. Others will respect cautiously given opinions.

Guest reflection post:

Day 5

YOU ARE COMPROMISING MY CUISINE

You will vomit up the little you have eaten and will have wasted your compliments. Do not speak to a fool, for he will scorn the wisdom of your words.

—Proverbs 23:8–9

Diary, day five. Hey, believer. If you can't swallow what I am saying, that's on you.

The writer speaks of the nauseating effect of trying to reason with a fool. His hideous approach to logic affects your digestive system, causing the inevitable. How do we recognize this individual since he has no visible warning labels? He has several very notable characteristics: he has an open mouth and a closed mind; he is usually too busy talking to listen; and he has all the answers to your unasked questions. Your words are mindless chatter for him to ridicule. How do you deal with him? Take heart. This is the only time God gives you permission to avoid someone.

Guest reflection post:

Day 6

THE FOOL HAS AN EMPTY BUCKET LIST

Fools fold their hands and ruin themselves.
—Ecclesiastes 4:5

Diary, day six. Hey, religious folks. Just wanted you to know "I get by with working as little as possible. I don't want to strain myself like those workaholics."

Did you not realize folding your hands was a sin? No! It is the implications. It is the smugness that says I will do what I want, when I want, and if I want. It symbolizes laziness, hands that are unwilling to make the slightest effort. It demonstrates defiance. "You cannot force me to do anything I don't want to do." It could also infer a lack of compassion. I chose to fold my hands rather than help others. Their end is the result of their disregard for any constructive effort. Because they do nothing, those who do are repulsive to them. They are stranded on a mental island surrounded by effort. The message is to unfold your hands, do whatever God puts in front of you, and enjoy the effort.

Why do fools despise knowledge?

Guest reflection post:

Day 7

THE FOOL IS A PRISONER OF MUSIC, BEHIND BARS WITH NO KEY

It is better to heed the rebuke of a wise person
than to listen to the song of fools.

—Ecclesiastes 7:5

Dear nosey book,

Day seven. Time to exercise my vocal cords. It's my personal song. I wrote it. Do you hear me singing? Listen and you might learn something.

Are you singing with the fools or just listening to the wind blow? Both have the same value. Neither are productive nor fruitful; however, a rebuke is intended to be a building block. The rebuker speaks to the rebukee to address their misconceptions. His intent is their growth. You can be offended by a rebuke, which benefits no one, or you can honestly evaluate it. I believe Solomon's desire is that we lead a productive life. To that end, he advises us to heed the critique of the experienced and invested. Do not let what is meant to tweak you, beat you.

Guest reflection post:

Week One

TIME FOR REFLECTION

Dear fool,

Just some thoughts I wanted to share with you. Your major premise and reasoning are flawed. We live in a world where much of our lives are based on that which we do not see. The wind blows and is only made visible by the trees. We breathe invisible oxygen, which keeps us alive. We cannot feel or touch the conscience, yet we see the results. The thinking process is invisible but so significant to our existence. They are all there, but you choose to ignore them. Open your heart and feel the invisible emotions of love. Embrace a child and feel what you cannot see. Please do not ask me to preach your funeral since you do not know where you are going. Neither do I.

Guest reflection post:

Day 8

HOW TO SHARPEN A FOOL

Though you *grind a fool* in a mortar, grinding him like grain with a pestle, you will not remove his folly from him.

—Proverbs 27:22

Dear diary,

I'm frustrated that "those people just don't realize my superior nature."

Many times, thoughtless and foolhardy people frustrate us. In our minds, we try to dissect them and understand what makes them tick. We grind them into the smallest bits to see if there is something inside them that will help us understand their behavior. Perhaps, if we can find the cause, there is hope for a cure. All our efforts are to no avail because their behavior is a choice, which they choose not to change. This means it is time to move on. If we value our time on earth, we must not squander it on those who do not value theirs.

Guest reflection post:

Day 9

LIFE IN THE FOOLISH LANE

How long will you who are simple love your simple ways? How long will mockers delight in mockery and fools hate knowledge?
—Proverbs 1:22

Dear diary,

Pardon me, I need a break from the fanatics. I am basking in the sunlight of my delusions.

The simple one is one who makes minimal effort to be involved in life. He revels in his apathetic approach by touting… "No one tells me what to do, I am my own person." He sits on his throne of ignorance and rules his domain of contempt. You will recognize him by his lack of interest in life. Do not let him frustrate you. He needs no advice. He will just ridicule what he does not understand. Live above the fray. Leave the simple ones to their own shame, and do not allow them to make you feel guilty. There are many serious persons who need and want your blessings.

Guest reflection post:

Day 10

THE FOOL USES MANY WORDS WITH NOTHING TO SAY

And fools *multiply words. No one knows what is coming—*
who can tell someone else what will happen after them?
—Ecclesiastes 10:14

Dear diary,

"There are roughly 470,000 words in the English language, and I know and use every one." I'm just not sure what I am saying or if they are listening.

One who multiplies words has no good intentions. His purpose is to confuse, to compromise truth, to frustrate judgments, or to fake understanding—all to protect himself. The problem is, he leaves others unprotected, uninformed, and unsure. Our response to excessive words is limited exposure. Listen only long enough to observe the absurdity and excessiveness. Realize there is no valid response. Do something constructive like straightening out your sock drawer.

Guest reflection post:

Day 11

The wise store up choice food and olive oil, but *fools gulp theirs down.*

—Proverbs 21:20

Hey, diary. Excuse me, I am writing in this digest while I am digesting and testing my intestines.

One who gulps does not savor, enjoy, or share. He eats to fill his belly. This is not bad by itself; however, what could be a feast becomes a routine meal. What applies to our intake of food could also apply to all areas of our life. We could be so engrossed in just filling in the blanks that we fail to enjoy all of life's blessings. God has designed life to be experienced and enjoyed. The fool gulps because his life lacks deep meaning. Do not be a gulper. Savor every moment of each day. Look for the depth of meaning attached to every event.

Guest reflection post:

Day 12

A wise son brings joy to his father, but a
foolish man despises his mother.

—Proverbs 15:20

Hey, diary. My parents don't have a clue. They just don't understand me.

Our parents are our ultimate supporters. From birth to infinity, their desire is our success and continued growth. When we stray into the abyss of folly, our parents and our God are betrayed. Our values are compromised, morals are ignored, and the future is sacrificed. The fool has total disregard and disrespect for his mother's dreams for her child. She carried him in her womb. She birthed him with her body and nourished him with her breasts. She hurts for his soul. You are the apple of your mother's eye. Give her the gift of your success. You will also make your daddy happy and your Father in heaven rejoice.

Day 13

He who walks with the wise grows wise, but
a companion of fools suffers harm.

—Proverbs 13:20

Dairy, follow me to a day of reckoning. I know exactly where I am going. I don't need a map. My GPS and I have a relationship.

Who you walk with will determine where you are going. If you walk with those whose direction is questionable, neither you nor they will know where they are going. You can't go where the wise are by following the foolish. You cannot go where the industrious are by following the lazy. You cannot go where the happy are by following the sad. You cannot go where the blessed are by following the doomed. You cannot go where God is by following the godless. You cannot go where the saved are by following the lost. You cannot go where the confident are by following the insecure. Who you are following today will determine where you will be tomorrow. Follow the wrong person and you will suffer the ultimate harm, the loss of the future.

Guest reflection post:

Day 14

If a wise man goes to court with a fool, the fool
rages and scoffs, and there is no peace.

—Proverbs 29:9

The court of life is continually in session. We are all on trial daily. A man's actions determine whether he is foolish or wise. Solomon gives a vivid picture of the fool. He rages because he thinks people will mistake his loudness for intelligence. The fool scoffs because all he knows is how to ridicule others and is devoid of facts; thus, if you try to prove your case to a fool or have it proven by a fool, you will just end up frustrated. When someone starts ranting and raving, the case is closed in his mind. Why contaminate your day with the reasoning of a fool? Take a long recess and enjoy the peace.

Guest reflection post:

Week Two

TIME FOR REFLECTION

Hey, Christian. Bigot life is easy for me. I do what I need to do to get by. Your Bible commands offend me. I won't worry about what you folks constantly worry about. I love to share my philosophy of life with you.

Dear fool,

You can hate what you do not understand or be challenged by it. God is a god of growth; therefore, he gives us true knowledge designed to perpetuate our growth. Those who shun his knowledge spurn opportunity; therefore, to save face, you will resort to ridicule. That is what you do best. By ridiculing, you lessen the value, demean the process, and put yourself on a pedestal. You rejoice over your ignorance. The question God has for you is, "*How long* will you wallow in perpetual ignorance and squander opportunity?" You have a choice. You can play the fool or peruse knowledge and rejoice on a higher plane.

Guest reflection post:

Day 15

For the waywardness of the simple will kill them,
and the *complacency of fools* will destroy them.

—Proverbs 1:32

Hey, diary. Hey, believer, this is my favorite attribute.

This proverb settles the issue, once and for all, as to who our worst enemy is. It is us. Self-destruction comes at the end of a life strewn with bad choices. The two major traps are waywardness and complacency. Waywardness is the willful defiance of the Almighty. This is characteristic of the simple individual who gives no thought to tomorrow or consequences. Complacency is a smug, self-satisfying, self-gratifying life dedicated to no one and nothing. This foolish person destroys himself by believing he needs no one or anything. The antidote—live a life in submission to God and in service to others.

Guest reflection post:

Day 16

Some *became fools through their rebellious ways* and suffered affliction because of their iniquities.

—Psalm 107:17

Hey, diary. I am comfortable making others uncomfortable.

Not all fools start out as fools. This verse is our primary warning to distance ourselves from the those who are rebellious, which can lead us to be foolhardy. We see some earn the title of fool by their actions or lack thereof. We must realize life consists of choices. Deciding our direction is our primary choice. We will choose to go either toward something or away from it. The person who makes the wrong choice suffers the consequence of their choices. Rebellious ways always have a backlash. We should choose the sensible route and eliminate the potential for indiscretion. At times, we all go through rebellious stages, but do not let yourself live with the fools.

Guest reflection post:

Day 17

Do not answer a fool according to his folly,
or you will be like him yourself.

—Proverbs 26:4

Hey, diary. I still haven't heard from my friends. This is day seventeen. I'm still waiting for their response.

When you answer a fool according to his folly, you respond to his desire to entrap you into his distorted way of thinking. By giving him the answer, he desires to a carefully calculated question. You give him credibility; thus, you will be like him. Also, when you respond in a reactionary or defensive way, you are allowing his question to control your answer. To avoid this, follow Solomon's advice, and give a gentle answer. A gentle answer keeps your emotions in check and puts you in control, whereas a harsh word builds your resentment and stirs his anger. Take charge of the day; give gentle answers.

Guest reflection post:

Day 18

Fools mock at making amends for sin, but
goodwill is found among the upright.

—Proverbs 14:9

Hey, diary. Who defines sin?

At times, it may seem easier to ignore a transgression than to make amends. The upright has no qualms about righting wrongs. In fact, they are anxious to do so. The fool's problem is his refusal to take responsibility. His mockery comes in the form of minimizing his indiscretion. By doing this, he keeps himself in bondage to his bad behavior. What he believes to be wise is evidence of his folly. The honest desires goodwill, which comes only by keeping all relationships right, especially one's relationship to God. Release yourself, tie up the loose ends, apologize if you need to, repent when necessary, and enjoy the rest of your life.

"Rise up, O God, and defend your cause; remember how *fools mock* you all day long. Do not ignore the clamor of your adversaries, the uproar of your enemies, which rises continually" (Psalm 74:22–23).

The reason fools mock God is because they cannot accept the challenge of believing in him. It is easier for them to clamor against him than to consider him. His moral absolutes threaten their lifestyle. King David is calling out to God to defend himself. He suggests God to not ignore the enemy. Maybe the king was misreading God. Could God's silence be speaking to the king and saying, "I am defending myself when I answer prayers, when the wind blows, when a newborn baby cries, and when a loved one peacefully closes their eyes and awaits their welcome home." God defends himself daily. Just look around you. The next time the winds blows, listen. God is whispering, "I love you."

Guest reflection post:

Day 19

The lips of the wise spread knowledge, but
the *hearts of fools are not upright.*

—Proverbs 15:7

Hey, diary. Time for my daily "whether" report. I don't know whether to listen or leave.

Our use of our lips can bring honor or dishonor. They can help, hurt, or heal. They can also friend, facilitate, or frustrate. You decide how you will use your words. If knowledge is your intent, you will choose positive and affirming words. Ultimately, your lips will honor our Creator and speak on his behalf. The fool is careless with his words. His lips only utter that which requires no thought or emotion. Since he is devoid of feelings, his words have no value. This day, use your God-given wisdom to simplify your life and enrich others.

Day 20

The toil of *fools* wearies them; they *do not know the way to town.*
—Ecclesiastes 10:15

Hey, diary. Call me anytime. I have a "toil-free" number. Some folks burn daylight. I burn my night-light.

Toil is fuel for the productive; however, it is a drudgery for the listless. If we find no pleasure in our life's vocation, it means we are either lazy, or it is not our calling. The results are a loss of direction and questioning our values. Time for constructive evaluation. First, decide what you want your life's legacy to be. What you want to be remembered for. Then put your hand to the plow, and do not even glance back. With all your might, make you dreams become realities.

Guest reflection post:

Day 21

The wisdom of the prudent is to give thought to
their ways, but the folly of *fools* is deception.

—Proverbs 14:8

Solomon gives us the key to wisdom when he describes the wise as one who "gives thought to their ways." One who gives thought to their ways takes seriously the direction they are going, the destination they desire, and the baggage they are carrying. All this must be considered before we can enjoy the benefits of God's wisdom. Contrary to that, the fool, who lives in the deceptive mode, deceives himself by ignoring the obvious. He has no direction, no destiny, and he enjoys his excess baggage. He believes it is his duty to carry and brag about it. The fool is going nowhere, carrying nothing for no reason.

Guest reflection post:

Week Three

TIME FOR REFLECTION

Hey, diary. Tell them not to talk about me.
Their churches are full of hypocrites.

Dear fool,

The one whom Jesus called a hypocrite in Matthew 7 was the one who was more aware of the other man's faults than his own. Therefore, the hypocrite defines his or her self when they focus more on the other person's shortcomings and ignore his or her own, just as you define yourself when you attempt to deceive. Next, we have a test to show who is foolish or wise.

"The way of a fool seems right to him, but a wise man listens to advice" (Proverbs 12:15).

The above is a test to see if you are foolish or wise. There are many reasons we do not listen to advice–for example, being too busy, planning to later, not wanting to know we are wrong, or having no time. All the excuses still do not make one any less a fool. The fool wears blinders, which limit his sight to what he knows. He loses the benefit of the experience and knowledge of others. There are times we earn the respect of others by giving them a listening ear. Listening to advice does not mean we have to take it. It does indicate we are objective and open-minded. Do we pass the test?

Guest reflection post:

Day 22

A discerning man keeps wisdom in view, but a *fool's eyes wander* to the ends of the earth.

—Proverbs 17:24

Hey, diary. I'm just looking around to see what's available. It's obvious that believers can't see what I see.

When it comes to what we see, there are three choices we have: the direction we look in, how long we look at something, and if we take a second look. The same is true with the mind's eye. The discerning individual knows he cannot always control what he sees when spanning the universe; however, he does know the above three choices are his. The foolish individual avoids making the three choices; he does not look at anything long enough or is not careful enough to grow. His eyes and mind continually wander. Keep in view only that which can be looked at and thought about in the company of God and others; this is the essence of wisdom.

Guest reflection post:

Day 23

Why *should fools have money* in hand to buy wisdom,
when they are not able to understand it?

—Proverbs 17:16

Money is the last thing you want to give the unresponsible. Trying to buy that which one cannot purchase is as foolish is it gets. This verse is just as applicable today as it was over two thousand years ago. Many today believe that money is the answer to all their problems. First, we should consider what money cannot buy before we ask what it will buy. This is where understanding begins. Remember, you can buy a house, but only love will make it a home. You can buy health insurance, but only God gives life.

Guest reflection post:

Day 24

Stone is heavy and sand a burden, but *provocation by a fool* is heavier than both.

—Proverbs 27:3

A fool's provocation has no good intention. It is his desire to leave you overloaded. Provocation is a fool's only talent. That is why he provokes. How do you respond to a fool's provocation? How do you revoke his provoke? One must realize the fool has a self-imposed diminished capacity; therefore, he cannot engage in constructive conversation. He will not compliment or encourage. Once you realize you are dealing with a fool, bid him *adieu*. The more you respond, the heavier the load becomes. Hand him back the load. If you still need a burden to carry, get two doughnuts, a cup of coffee, and feel guilty.

Guest reflection post:

Day 25

When you make a vow to God, do not delay to fulfill it. He has no pleasure in *fools*; fulfill your vow.

—Ecclesiastes 5:4

A vow is a sacred pledge. The passage is clarifying the seriousness and implications of making a vow, especially to God. So often we privately and mentally make a commitment to the Father. If I make it through this, or if I get that, I will. First, realize that just because a vow is not written or spoken, it is still an obligation. Next, a vow is not commanded or necessary. It is a personal decision; therefore, if we make a vow, it is foolhardy not to keep it. The foolishness is in believing we can manipulate God or others by flippantly giving them what they want. Value your words. Cherish each syllable and take responsibility for them. When you follow through, you will have taken a step closer to God.

Guest reflection post:

Day 26

Remember how the enemy has mocked you, LORD,
how foolish people *have reviled your name.*

—Psalm 74:18

Hey, diary. I don't need their version of God, grace, and Jesus. I just need my version—*me*.

To disrespect the Almighty is to disrespect his creation; therefore, we should take very personally the fool's mockery. The name of our benefactor is too precious to be ridiculed. This form of disrespect shows the ignorance of those who choose it. They assault that which they do not make any effort to understand. This seems to give them a twisted form of satisfaction as they search for a claim to fame. We can loathe or learn from the fool. That which is valued by others should be given due respect. The name of the Almighty must be revered by all always.

Guest reflection post:

Day 27

Like the crackling of thorns under the pot, so is the laughter of *fools*. This too is meaningless.

—Ecclesiastes 7:6

Hey, diary. Where is God when they needed him? *Ha ha*, that's on them.

Laughter is a gift from God. When used to lighten a situation and lift up spirits, it is blessing. When laughter is used to ridicule, mock, or humiliate, it a fiendish instrument. This is how the fool uses laughter. His purpose is to belittle individuals and co-opt situations. His laughter is relentless. It resonates and irritates. It benefits no one, not even the fool. If you feel the need to laugh at someone, be sure you are laughing with them and not at them. Enjoy every gift from God. Never misuse emotions that he has intended to be a blessing.

Guest reflection post:

Day 28

Even as *fools* walk along the road, they lack sense
and show everyone how stupid they are.

—Ecclesiastes 10:3

Because the fool lives in a fog, he is isolated from truth; therefore, he creates his own reality. To find acceptance, he goes through life talking more than thinking or listening. Fools hide nothing to their chagrin and embarrassment. Their folly is easily recognized. They have no control, no respect, and no judgment. If you choose to join them, put your brain in neutral and your mouth in overdrive. What he thinks is proclamation is isolation. Be safe, be focused, and be sure you are not on the fool's radar. Do not get to close to him. He is outrageous and contagious.

Guest reflection post:

Day 29

Words from the mouth of the wise are gracious,
but fools are *consumed by their own lips*.

—Ecclesiastes 10:12

Words are the portals of the universe. One must use them with extreme caution. With words, we save, help, encourage, build, connect, lead, follow, destroy…oops! I went the wrong way. Words are either good or bad. There are no generics. How we use them makes the difference. The wise person values his words and uses them thoughtfully. Gracious words are used to connect, sarcastic words are used to alienate, and academic words are used to inform. The foolish misuse of words compromises their user by revealing their ignorance and ill intentions. Use your words with good intentions. Remember, they will linger a lifetime.

Guest reflection post:

Day 30

He who *trusts in himself is a fool*, but he
who walks in wisdom is kept safe.

—Proverbs 28:26

Hey, diary. If I could find my bootstraps, I would pull myself up.

Self-trust can be very deceptive because it is more emotional than rational. This passage is not an indictment against initiative or confidence. It is encouraging willingness for evaluation and a desire to grow. A fool cannot bear the thought that someone may know more than him. He risks everything to prove nothing. We play it safe and keep our regrets to a minimum when we seek the advice and counsel of those who are more experienced. Others will respect us for asking, and we will respect ourselves for not being too pretentious. Have a safe week.

Guest reflection post:

The Final Reflection

The way of a fool seems right to him, but
a wise man listens to advice.

—Proverbs 12:15

The above is a test to see if you are foolish or wise. There are many reasons we do not listen to advice—for example, being too busy, planning to later, not wanting to know we are wrong, or having no time. All the excuses still do not make one any less a fool. The fool wears blinders, which limit his sight to what he knows. He loses the benefit of the experience and knowledge of others. There are times we earn the respect of others by giving them a listening ear. Listening to advice does not mean we have to take it. It does indicate we are objective and open-minded. Do we pass the test?

Guest reflection post your final thoughts:

Summary

Please continue to consider the intent of this book and of the scriptures. By understanding foolish actions, attitudes, and aspirations, we release ourselves to grow. We are not in bondage to our emotions. We grow by not engaging in activities that are foolhardy and without direction.

Love,
Johnny D.

Possible Guest Reflections Posts

I need to work on...
I need to change...
That works for me...
Poor fool...
I don't understand them...
I believe because...
That's what I thought...
We need to understand the fool...
He just needs a little love...
Someone is delusional...
You think...
Takes too much time...
Someone is enjoying their ignorance...
I need to change friends...
I recognize him...
You know me to well...
Rock their world...

About the Author

John P. DiMarzio Sr. (Chaplain Johnny D.) began his ministry by moving his family into the church basement forty-nine years ago. Since then, he has pastored four different churches over forty-one years. After retiring from the ministry, he began serving as chaplain for Ashton Creek Health and Rehabilitation Center and as a staff chaplain for Parkview Regional Medical Center. He also continues to serve as a shepherd with the Southwind Church of Christ, which he and others planted. He and his wife, Kathy, have fostered forty-one children as well as rising their five children. He is now blessed with eleven grandchildren.

After serving a tour in the US Marine Corps, then becoming a machinist for eight years, and after much prayer, he entered the ministry. He has also served many organizations starting out as a volunteer fireman. From there, he has volunteered as director, counselor, and session leader for several youth camps. He became an advocate for grieving children and facilitator for pregnancy and relationship resources center. He has also interviewed and assisted clients for a community benevolence program.

He has a bachelor of science in psychology degree from Carolina University of Theology and master of ministries degree from Bethel College. He has written two other books as well as articles for newspapers, various periodicals, and weekly newsletters.